How often have you said 'I nearly died laughing'? Incredible as it may seem, in March 1975 someone actually did! Alexander Mitchell collapsed and died after laughing non-stop for half-an-hour at his favourite television comedy programme.

Even on their death-beds, some people manage to retain their sense of humour. Sir Noel Coward departed this life with the words 'Goodnight my darlings, I'll see you tomorrow.' Some last words are inadvertently humorous — as the audience chuckled at a joke at the end of his act, Tommy Cooper ad-libbed 'I thought it would get a bigger laugh than that.' It was the last joke he ever made.

This hilarious collection of last moments from all the corners of the globe proves that even in death there can, on occasions, be a touch of humour.

DIED LAUGHING
Or,
One Last Goodbye!

RICHARD DE'ATH

London
UNWIN PAPERBACKS
Boston   Sydney

First published by Unwin Paperbacks 1985

UNWIN ® PAPERBACKS
40 Museum Street, London WC1A 1LU, UK

Unwin Paperbacks
Park Lane, Hemel Hempstead, Herts HP2 4TE, UK

George Allen & Unwin Australia Pty Ltd
8 Napier Street, North Sydney, NSW 2060, Australia

Unwin Paperbacks with the Port Nicolson Press
PO Box 11-838 Wellington, New Zealand

© Richard De'ath, 1985

ISBN 0 04 827149 7

Set in 11 on 12 point Clearface by
A. J. Latham Ltd., Dunstable
and printed in Great Britain by
Cox & Wyman Ltd., Reading

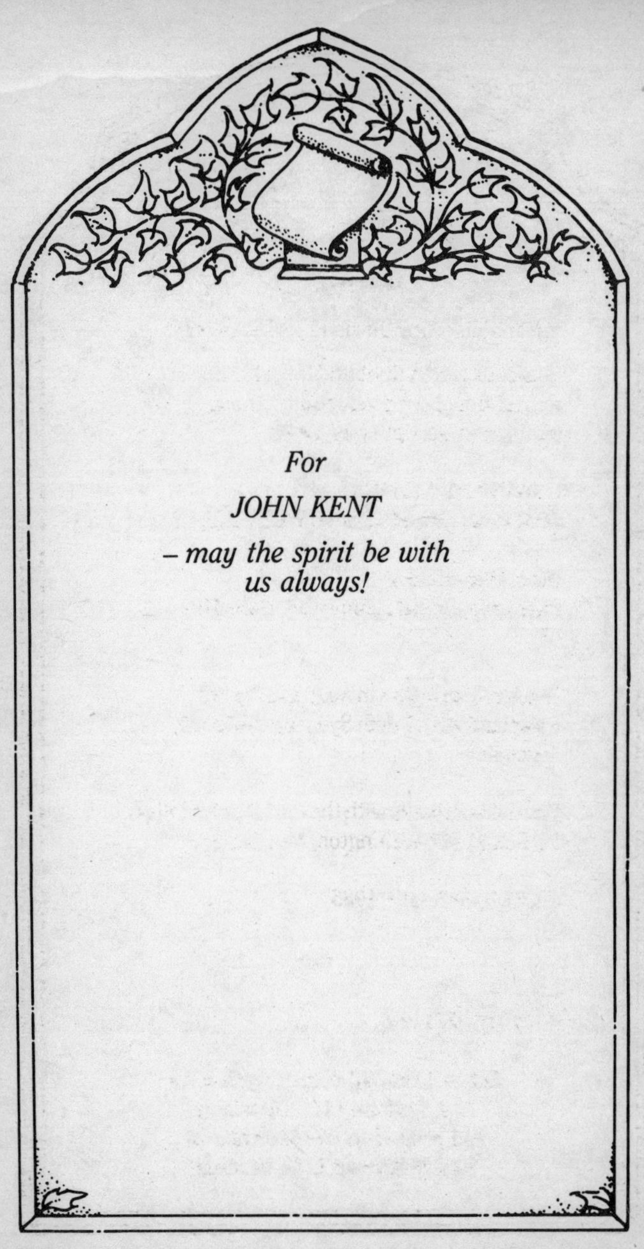

For

JOHN KENT

*– may the spirit be with
us always!*

CONTENTS

PREFACE

You've probably heard the joke about the man who died laughing – well, it actually came true in March 1975. A jovial Scotsman named Alexander Mitchell got such a chuckle from his favourite television comedy programme, 'The Goodies', that it killed him.

His wife Nessie explained afterwards that one of the sketches which involved a fight between a black pudding and some bagpipes had set Alex off.

'It tickled my husband and he just kept laughing non-stop throughout the whole half-hour programme,' she said. 'It was nearly over when he collapsed.'

Mrs Mitchell told the press that she bore the comedians concerned no hard

feelings – in fact she was even going to write to them thanking them for making her husband's last minutes so happy! And she added, 'I have often said, "I nearly died laughing", but I never thought it could happen. It is incredible.'

Incredible it certainly is. But though death is invariably sad, it sometimes comes, as in this case, with a touch of humour. And that in a nutshell (or a coffin, if you prefer) is what this collection of last moments is all about. For herein you will find a lot of dead funny tales that I have collected from all over the world and spanning the past eighty odd years. (I've stuck to the twentieth century to avoid a volume the size of the *Domesday Book*.) They range from the actual moment of passing to some pretty ghastly interventions from the spirit world. Each story has also given the person concerned a little slice of immortality – for it should be stressed that every one of them is true!

Sometimes the humour is almost unintentional – like the case in

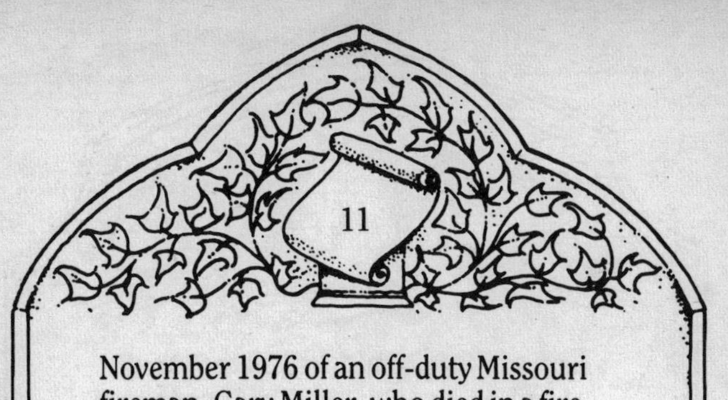

November 1976 of an off-duty Missouri fireman, Gary Miller, who died in a fire which broke out in his home while he was asleep. In the ruins of his house was found a smoke detector which had obviously been awaiting installation. It was ringing dutifully.

Sometimes it is of a much blacker kind as in the instance of a 30-year-old Florida TV newsreader, Miss Chris Chubbock, who suddenly announced on her programme in July 1974, 'In keeping with Channel 40's policy of bringing you the latest in blood and guts and in living colour, you are now going to see another first – attempted suicide.' With this, Miss Chubbock pulled a gun from under her desk and shot herself in the head. She died fourteen hours later without regaining consciousness.

And on still other occasions it reaches the level of pure farce. I quote the story of the ham-fisted French safe-cracker who was shot and killed by gendarmes after a night of trying to break into a Paris bank safe in 1978. Only afterwards was it discovered that the safe had been

accidentally left unlocked all the time!

Just occasionally, too, the jaws of death don't quite snap shut – and you end up with hilarious instances like the group of Chinese refugees who tried to commit suicide in 1982 after being refused permission to settle in the Philippines. Rather than return home, the men poured over themselves what they thought to be petrol and then tried to set it on fire. Only after several matches had been unavailingly applied to the 'petrol' was it discovered that it was, in fact, fish sauce!

Of course, there have also been some very amusing last words from people on their death beds, and I believe that a section of the best of these warrants a place in this book. And add to them some of the quite hilarious words of valediction pronounced on the not-always-so-dear-departed by those involved in their passing and you have a laugh-a-page assembly about that one moment we *all* have to face one day.

From these remarks I am sure you will gather that my book is a pot-pourri

of dying moments that also happen to be very much a laughing matter. Together I think they prove that even where there is death there can still be a touch of humour. (If not, you'll know this is one De'ath to avoid on the cover of future books!)

So, if you will, please enjoy One Last Goodbye. . .

Richard De'Ath
October 1984

1

WORSE TO COME

'There's worse to come' has proved literally and often grimly true, and there are few better examples with which to begin a section of the more outlandish cases of this kind, than the story of Major Walter Summerford.

In 1918, while fighting in Flanders, Major Summerford was struck by lightning, thrown from his horse, and as a result of his injuries was invalided out of the Army.

Six years later, back in his native Canada, he was hit again by lightning while fishing near Vancouver. And in 1930 all the odds about lightning never striking twice, let alone three times, were overturned when *another* bolt struck him and left him paralysed!

Major Summerford died in 1932 and

was laid to rest in a secluded grave not far from Vancouver. Then, two years later, nature played her final trick — a shaft of lightning struck the poor Major's grave and completely shattered his headstone!

*   *   *

During an outbreak of fighting at an isolated outpost on the Mons front also during the First World War, a German soldier named Heinz Müller shot and killed an English soldier in the opposing trenches.

Later, as Müller advanced with some other German troops to the English lines, he found the body of the man he had killed still upright, his rifle aimed to fire and his now cold finger still poised on the trigger.

Deciding to take the dead man's rifle as a souvenir of his success, Müller

wrestled with the stiff fingers to release the weapon. As he did so, the rifle suddenly went off and shot him dead through the heart!

*   *   *

When Abe Bonham, a sharecropper of Cotter in Arkansas, returned from a shopping trip in August 1928 he saw smoke billowing from his small wooden home.

Quickly, Abe recruited help from other sharecroppers living nearby and with their assistance was able to salvage a good many items from the burning building, as well as finally bringing the flames under control.

Just before the fire was put out, however, there was a sudden report. A gun which Abe always kept loaded in the drawer of a bureau had been set off by the flames.

And, tragically, it was Abe who was in the way of the stray bullet — he fell dead at the feet of his friends.

*   *   *

As David Anthony was driving home to Liverpool in March 1936, he suddenly came around a sharp bend and found to his horror another car racing towards him on the wrong side of the road.

Desperately, David slammed on his brakes, but his car skidded uncontrollably and the two vehicles collided head on.

When David regained consciousness in hospital, he was thankful to learn he had escaped the terrible accident with only minor cuts and bruises. The other motorist, too, had also miraculously survived.

But there had been a passenger in the other car and he was dead. And the

unfortunate man turned out to be David
Anthony's twin brother, Paul . . .

*   *   *

Some weeks after Igor Ravenko had
undergone a stomach operation in
Moscow in 1949, he returned to hospital
complaining of more abdominal pains.
For a second time he was operated on,
and the medical team discovered the
previous surgeon had inadvertently left a
pair of clamps in Igor's stomach.

Happy at this discovery, Igor returned
to his family. A month later the poor
fellow was dead.

At the autopsy he was opened up once
more. And this time in his stomach was
discovered a surgical gauze pad which
the second surgeon had left behind!

*   *   *

20

Luigi Ercolli chose the most horrendous way of committing suicide in 1959 — he decided to set fire to himself on a deserted headland not far from his home in Nardo, southern Italy.

No sooner had he begun his grisly ritual, however, than Luigi had second thoughts. Frantically, he began to roll about on the ground and beat at the flames.

In his terror, though, he forgot where he was — and suddenly fell over the edge of the headland and plunged to his death on the rocks below. . .

*   *   *

The most bizarre case of a near fatal motoring accident occurred in the Ténéré desert in the Niger, in 1960.

A French soldier, Henri Le Queux, was driving an army lorry across this vast, sandy wilderness when he rammed

a tree and overturned the vehicle.
Reports said he was lucky to escape with
his life.

The tree was the only one within a
radius of fifteen miles!

*　　　*　　　*

A persistent lover in Hamburg, West
Germany, refused to heed warnings
about the crazy lengths to which he was
going to impress his loved one.

He would clamber over roofs to see
her. Shin over high walls merely to catch
a glimpse. And even hang from wires
outside the office where she worked.

In July 1963, the exasperated police
finally gave chase when they spotted the
boy on the roof of the girl's home. As he
ran, the youth suddenly slipped and fell
75 feet down a chimney.

A few minutes later he was found with
his neck broken – lying in the fireplace of
his girl's bedroom.

While suffering from acute depression, Walter Alexander, a Chicago engineer, drove to a local motel in March 1966 intent on committing suicide. In one of the bedrooms he took out a revolver and shot himself three times in the head.

Some hours later Walter awoke to find he was still alive and feeling rather better. He decided to return home and tell his wife the injuries to his head had been caused by a fall. Miraculously, all three bullets had passed straight through his head.

A week later, however, Walter received a visit from the police. They had found the three bullets from his revolver in the wall of the motel bedroom.

On admitting to his incredible escape from death, he was promptly charged with causing criminal damage.

*   *   *

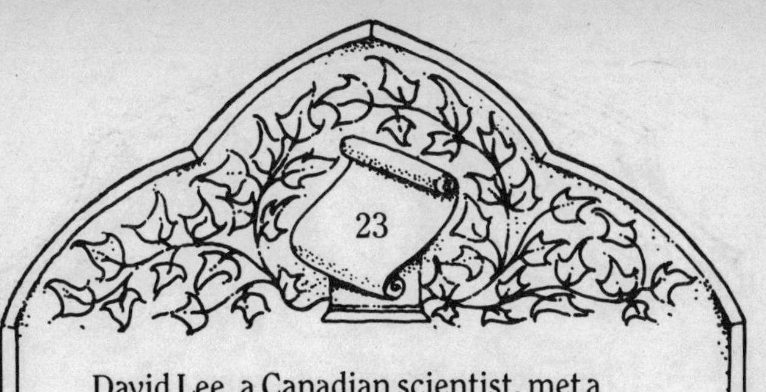

David Lee, a Canadian scientist, met a tragic end in 1967, when he was decapitated because he did not bend low enough as he was climbing into a helicopter and had his head cut off by the rotor blades.

Later, the case came to court – and the Quebec magistrates ruled that Lee's estate must pay for the damage done to the helicopter!

*   *   *

Californian Carol Hargis set out with dedicated and ingenious efficiency to kill her unfortunate husband, Harry, in 1968.

First, she gave him a massive dose of LSD. This did no more than give him a mind-bending trip.

Next, she dosed a blackberry pie with the venom of a tarantula – but still he survived.

24

Equally unsuccessful was sabotaging his car with a home-made bomb (it failed to go off) and attaching a live electric wire to his shower.

Once again she returned to poor Harry's food – dosing his beer with tranquilisers, but he thought the drink was off and threw it away. When he fell ill from all these unpleasant attentions, Carol even tried injecting air into his veins.

She finally succeeded in her objective – and earned a life sentence – by the simple expedient of striking him on the head with an iron bar.

*　　*　　*

Tired of all the violence in the streets of her native Belfast, Mrs Elizabeth McClelland emigrated around the world to New Zealand in 1970.

Tragically, just two years later, in

February 1972, Mrs McClelland was rushed into a Christchurch hospital suffering from head injuries from which she subsequently died.

Police inquiries established that her injuries had been caused by being struck on the head by a placard carried by a demonstrator who was protesting on behalf of Irish Civil Rights.

*   *   *

The death penalty is applied for several crimes in Saudi Arabia – persistent theft being one of them.

A young burglar in the town of Jiddah was prepared to take the risk when he thought he had found a foolproof way to beat the security bars on the windows of a luxury block of flats. So, in March 1972, in order to get through these bars, he took off all his clothes and his shoes.

Inside the apartment block, however,

the naked youth was suddenly surprised by a returning resident and had to flee. His initial delight at having avoided an appointment with the executioner by his cleverness suddenly turned to horror, though, when a thought flashed into his mind.

In the pocket of the trousers he had left behind . . . his identity card!

*   *   *

After his wife had left him, John Stratton of Manchester saw no point in going on living. He decided to commit suicide in 1973, and having carefully sealed the doors and windows of his home, turned on the gas oven.

Although the fumes soon engulfed the house, because the supply was North Sea gas, it proved non-toxic. This lucky escape made Stratton have second thoughts.

Perhaps he would give life another chance. He took a cigar from the mantelpiece and lit it.

At this, the highly inflammable North Sea gas exploded him and his house into smithereens.

*   *   *

David Falconer had been growing ever more depressed during the months of 1974. And it seemed to make no difference what his friend Sharon Payne did or suggested — he grew still more gloomy.

Then, one night as the couple sat in Falconer's Los Angeles apartment, he pulled a pistol from under a cushion, thrust it against his temple, and pulled the trigger.

The horrified Sharon could only watch in terror as the bullet killed her friend, passed through his head,

ricocheted off a wall, and then struck her right between the eyes. She never recovered consciousness.

* * *

As Woodrow Creekmore was driving to his home in Chickasha, Oklahoma, in 1976, his car suddenly slewed across the road and hit a telegraph pole. Amazingly, he was able to get out of the virtually demolished vehicle without a scratch.

However, as he stood discussing the accident with a police patrolman who appeared on the scene, the telegraph pole suddenly toppled over and, striking Woodrow on the head, killed him instantly.

* * *

In February 1976, a Belgian doctor, Herman le Compte, claimed that he had devised a rejuvenation treatment which would enable people to live for 1,000 years.

The police were not impressed by his statement that he was able to arrest the natural deterioration of the body's organs by massive injections and exercise – and arrested him. He was placed in jail in Bruges to await trial for practising medicine while debarred.

Then while he waited, 'Dr Long Life' – as he was nicknamed – suffered a heart attack . . .

*   *   *

When Billy Vecchio of Chicago stole a car to impress his girlfriend in August 1976, he ended up with a very different ride from the one he had expected.

During his little outing, the car broke

down and Vecchio hailed a passer-by to
give him a push. The man, Joe White,
just happened to be the real owner of the
car!

Vecchio, however, laughed at the
other man's claim and proceeded to
punch White, a night-club bouncer by
profession, on the nose.

Before he repossessed his vehicle –
White later explained to a local court –
he broke both Vecchio's wrists, fractured
his jaw, and then stabbed him. The
joy-rider subsequently died of his
injuries.

*   *   *

According to the *Detroit Free Press*, in
July 1977, Mr Michael Maryn of Passaic
in New Jersey had been mugged
eighty-three times during the previous
five years.

He had been shot twice, stabbed,
coshed, lost part of one ear, had his nose

broken, his ribs smashed and his skull fractured. In addition to his injuries, he had lost numerous bags of groceries, four cars and over $2,000 in cash.

'I don't worry about it,' Mr Maryn told the newspaper, 'I'm lucky in one respect – I have a blood clot in my leg that keeps me from travelling far from home.'

*   *   *

An Italian named Abel Ruiz felt the world had ended when he was jilted in June 1978.

In his despair he hurled himself in front of the Genoa–Madrid Express. But, miraculously, he fell between the rails and sustained only minor injuries.

After being treated at the Genoa hospital, the self-destructive Abel tried suicide a second time. This time he leapt in front of a lorry. Again, he was only slightly injured by the impact.

Following further treatment at the hospital, he was only released on the understanding that he would not try to kill himself again.

But, within the hour, he was back once more. This time, though, the incident was a genuine accident: he had been struck by a runaway horse. And now his injuries *were* serious.

The following day the man who wanted to commit suicide was dead — accidentally!

* * *

After weeks of excruciating pain from toothache, a market trader from Leeds named Walter Hallas could stand it no more. But his fear of dentists was such that he could not bring himself to seek expert help.

Instead, in December 1979, Walter went to one of his workmates and asked

him to punch him in the jaw in the hope that would dislodge the offending molar.

The punch did just that. But Walter was also knocked over by the blow, struck his head on the ground as he fell, and died of a fractured skull.

* * *

Like many people, Herman Holt worried about his income tax. Indeed, when the 55-year-old chip shop owner from Halifax, Australia, received a letter from the Revenue in 1980, he became convinced he had fallen foul of the authorities and decided to kill himself rather than face disgrace. The following day he was found dead by a railway line.

In actual fact the letter had nothing to do with arrears – it was the Revenue admitting they owed *him* A$1,400!

* * *

For several years, Herbert Foster, a chemist in Auckland, New Zealand, campaigned to have a pedestrian crossing immediately in front of his shop re-sited. He argued that the position was a 'potential death trap' and that someone would surely be killed.

They were. On 19 October 1980, just a week after Herbert had delivered yet another tirade about it in the local paper, he himself used it to cross the road and was struck and killed by a passing car!

* * *

After months of trying to find a job, Romolo Ribolla, grew so dejected he decided to kill himself. On the morning of 4 April 1981, as he sat in the kitchen of his home near Pisa, he suddenly produced a gun from his pocket and told his wife he was going to shoot himself.

For nearly an hour, the distraught

woman pleaded with Romolo until, overcome with emotion at her entreaties, he burst into tears and flung the revolver to the floor.

But as it struck the ground, the gun went off and shot Mrs Ribolla dead.

*   *   *

A man described as 'The Most Accident-Prone Person in Britain' made a habit of spending every Friday the thirteenth in bed for his own safety, according to a report published in November 1981.

For in the space of five years, Robert Renphrey, a Peterborough bus driver, had suffered one calamity after another on this fateful Friday. He had been:
Involved in five car crashes and four bus breakdowns.
Fallen into a river and been knocked down by a motorcycle.
And even walked through a plate glass door!

Giuseppe Saraniti was convinced his wife was having an affair with Salvatore Manganaro. And in March 1983 he confronted the other man in his home in Genoa, Italy, brandishing a revolver.

Falling to his knees, Salvatore swore that the story was not true. He had never touched Maria Saraniti. But Giuseppe was not convinced and thrust the revolver against the frightened man's temple.

Salvatore closed his eyes and clutched at the gold pendant of the Virgin Mary hanging around his neck. 'Mother of Jesus,' he pleaded, 'give him a sign I am telling the truth.'

Giuseppe pulled the trigger. But nothing happened, only a dull click.

Now it was Giuseppe's turn to be frightened and he ran to the police station in Genoa and confessed what he had tried to do. After he had been charged with attempted murder, a police spokesman said, 'The strange thing was there was nothing wrong with the gun. It was fully loaded and worked perfectly when we tested it!'

Vittoria Luise loved his little three-wheeled bubble car and firmly believed it was his good luck charm – a much safer vehicle to ride in than ordinary cars. And on 6 February 1983, as he was driving alongside the river Sele near Naples, he had reason to believe his faith was well founded.

For a sudden gust of wind caught the little car and bowled it over into the river. Before it struck the water, however, the door flew open and Vittoria was flung clear, to be able to swim safely back to the bank.

Once on dry land, he was just congratulating himself on his narrow escape – though bemoaning the loss of his precious car – when another gust of wind blew a nearby tree down on top of him, killing him instantly.

*   *   *

A man aptly named Hi Woe was rushed naked into a hospital in Peking in

February 1983 with a metal spittoon stuck on his head.

According to the ambulancemen who brought him in, the spittoon—a common item in Chinese bedrooms—had been playfully plonked on his head by his wife while the couple were making love.

Although the doctors battled hard to save the young man's life, he died of asphixiation before he could be freed. Later, it was learned the previous evening had been his wedding night!

*　　*　　*

Mike Stewart, the president of the Auto Convoy Company in Dallas, Texas, was so convinced of the dangers that a number of low-level bridges in the city presented to traffic, that in April 1983 he decided to make a movie about the problem to convince the authorities.

Hiring a camera crew, he proceeded to drive around Dallas on the back of one of his trucks to film the potential death spots. As he did so, the truck went underneath one of the bridges in question and he was decapitated.

*   *   *

An attractive 16-year-old Israeli girl was taken to court in Tel Aviv in September 1983 and ordered to stop walking around her home in the nude.

The complainant was not a neighbour, but the girl's 80-year-old stepfather. Her provocative displays were to give him a heart attack, he said, so that she could inherit his fortune!

*   *   *

George Schwartz was a conscientious worker and with Christmas coming up, he decided on the evening of 10 December 1983 to put in some extra hours at his factory in Providence, Rhode Island.

Suddenly, as he worked, a huge explosion ripped the factory apart, and by a miracle George was thrown clear by the force of the blast. As he crawled away, he saw through the falling masonry and flames that only one wall of the factory was still upright.

After being treated for his injuries and shock, dedicated George returned to the remains of the factory to see if he could salvage any of the papers and files he had been working on.

As he was rooting through the debris, that sole surviving wall collapsed and crushed him to death.

*   *   *

41

Football fan Felix Gill was not enjoying watching his team Athletico Madrid play on 7 March 1984. For a start, the 70-year-old had had a row with his wife about going to the game.

Now Madrid were taking a beating at the hands (and feet) of their old rivals from Barcelona.

Then poor Felix slumped into a coma with a brain haemorrhage.

And there he stayed in his seat for *a day and a half* before he was discovered and rushed to hospital!

* * *

A shopping trip for a little old West German housewife in the city of Wuppertal in July 1984 turned into a catastrophe.

Having made her purchases, Frau Martha Harbou returned to her car. She smiled to herself at the sight of her pet

cat still asleep on the back seat where she had left her.

But no sooner had she began to drive off, however, than the cat suddenly leapt up and bit her. Frau Harbou screamed and lost control of the car.

At once the car careered into a parked lorry and then demolished a sausage stand. This, in turn, dragged a fish-frying stand over, burning an assistant with boiling fat. Pedestrians everywhere scattered as Frau Harbou's car finally smashed into a wall.

The unfortunate lady died shortly afterwards in hospital. The cat escaped without a scratch.

*   *   *

A French couple appeared in court at Bobigny near Paris in September 1984 charged with trying to murder each other.

43

The 60-year-old husband had been awoken suddenly in the night by a severe electric shock. Leaning over the bed was his wife, who was wearing rubber gloves and had attached an extension lead from the mains to his head. Over his heart a wet sheet had been laid.

Leaping from the bed, the man rushed to the next room, seized a rifle, and returned to shoot his wife in the thigh.

In court, it was explained that the man's poor eyesight had saved the life of the wife. And the electric shock had failed to kill him because the couple lived in one of the few streets in the area where Electricité de France provided a lower-powered system with less than the normal 220 volts which *would* have proved fatal!

*   *   *

2

FATEFUL TALES

Fate has played some cruel – and deadly – tricks on mankind. Take the case of New Yorker Joseph O'Malley. He was exceedingly drunk one night in 1953 and decided to take a short cut home along a subway railway line.

When, inevitably, nature called, O'Malley decided to pee right where he stood. Unfortunately, when the stream of urine hit the third rail of the track, 600 volts shot up into his body and he dropped dead.

*　　　*　　　*

While working on a farm near Ahmedabad in western India, in 1957, a

labourer accidentally fell into a deep storage pit full of cow manure.

Six other labourers who also jumped into the pit to try to rescue the man suffered the same fate — suffocation.

* * *

Because thieves were constantly stealing apples from her orchard, Mrs Laura Baines of Penzance in Cornwall decided to employ a nightwatchman to keep an eye out for the pilferers.

Unfortunately, Mrs Baines did not trust her employee and one night in 1959 she crept out into the orchard to make sure he was not asleep on the job.

The man shot her dead.

* * *

An elderly Swedish pastor met an unlikely end while engaged on church duties in the winter of 1955.

Pastor Karlo Toivio was baptising some new members of his church at the time – standing in a pool of heated water for the ceremony. Things went fatally wrong when his assistant clergyman handed him a live microphone . . .

*   *   *

Devoted birdwatcher Henry Humphret of New York was finding extreme difficulty in 1963 in getting near enough to some swans living on High Shield Lake to ring them. In desperation, he decided to try to approach them by night *in disguise*.

Obtaining the hollowed-out body of a swan, he placed it over his head and waded into the lake just after midnight. Unfortunately he could not swim and drowned in the darkness.

An eccentric Californian inventor, Reuben Tice, of Monterey, was obsessed with creating a machine for taking the wrinkles out of prunes.

In November 1967, having perfected a piece of equipment which he hoped would perform such a task, he set it in motion. A mighty explosion followed.

Tice was discovered dead under the shattered remains of his machine and a huge pile of prunes. They were all still wrinkled.

*   *   *

Horror struck the Brazilian town of Goiânia in December 1973 when a column of killer ants a mile long and half a mile wide marched into the community. It took sixty firemen with flame throwers over fifteen hours to drive the ants back into the jungle.

In their wake they left the scant

remains of several people they had
devoured – including the chief of police.

* * *

So distraught did Mrs Vera Czermak of
Prague become over her husband's
infidelities that she decided to commit
suicide from the window of her
third-floor flat. On the morning of 25
July 1975 she hurled herself out . . .
. . . and landed on Mr Czermak who
was returning unexpectedly to the flat.
She survived unhurt – he was killed.

* * *

Another man killed by an unlikely falling
object was Araldo Anastasi, a pensioner,

who was returning home to his
fourth-floor apartment on Rome's Via
dello Scalo, in February 1954.

Waiting excitedly for his return was
his little terrier dog, Leo, who yelped
with pleasure at a window when the old
man came into sight in the street below.

Unfortunately the little creature
overbalanced, fell from the ledge, and
landed on top of his master – killing him
outright.

*   *   *

Wishing to enhance her tan, American
sunbather Mrs Linda Saverd lay out on a
sheet of aluminium foil stretched over a
chaise-longue at her New Jersey home,
in August 1975. The idea was that the foil
would intensify the sun's rays.

It did – and Mrs Saverd cooked herself
to death in a temperature of nearly 110
degrees Fahrenheit.

A freak storm ended six years of drought in the Spanish Sahara in August 1975, leaving behind it a number of giant pools of water.

Into one of these, Mohammed Aliud fell and died – drowned in the middle of the desert.

*   *   *

Felix Hanaud, a 77-year-old Frenchman who had always received excellent medical care during his lifetime, decided to donate his body to science by giving it to the Toulouse University Medical Faculty.

In February 1976, some years after he had drawn up his will, Felix went into the University building, told the caretaker he could wait no longer – and shot himself through the head.

*   *   *

51

There was nothing that General Miguel Arracha, the head of the Anti-Urban Guerrilla Section of the Argentine Army, enjoyed more than a game of dominoes. Indeed, it was his habit to play each week at his home in Buenos Aires with a friend, General Carlos Mendoza.

But this came to an abrupt end in June 1976 when General Arracha was blown to pieces by a bomb that his friend General Mendoza left behind after one of their games!

*   *   *

Cricket has long been one of the great passions of the people of Pakistan, but in 1976 this passion got completely out of bounds during a match between two rival teams in the north of the country.

One of the umpires, Karim Singh, gave a number of decisions which were highly controversial and caused the

tempers of the fielding side to rise to the point of rage.

When, once again, Singh refused a clear-cut appeal for leg before wicket, several of the fielders grabbed the stumps from either end of the pitch and furiously beat the umpire to death!

*   *   *

Thoughts of love and romance were on the mind of honeymooner Philip Ryan as he walked back to his holiday cottage on Reunion Island in the Indian Ocean, in June 1977. He had taken a short stroll in the moonlight while his bride of one day was preparing for bed.

With a gleeful love call Philip vaulted over what he believed to be the fence surrounding the cottage – and disappeared into the crater of the Ganga volcano.

Keen angler José Hermanez accidentally struck a bees nest with his line while fishing from the banks of the Rio Negro not far from Sao Paolo, in August 1977. The infuriated bees immediately attacked Jose.

To escape, he leapt into the river – and was promptly devoured by piranha fish.

* * *

After undergoing a successful operation to have a replacement heart in November 1977, Mr George Least, a dairyman of Salisbury, Rhodesia, fell in love with a nurse who helped him through his convalescence.

When the girl did not return his love, Mr Least shot himself.

* * *

Former actress Eleanor Barry, 70, could not resist hoarding every newspaper, press cutting, book and souvenir which in any way related to her career. Over the years, this collecting mania grew to such an extent that the house she shared with her sister in New York became jammed from floor to ceiling.

On 20 December 1977, she was found dead in the house – a huge pile of the books and newspapers had fallen on her.

*   *   *

Charged with aiding a suicide, salesman Marvin Redland told a curious story to a court in Norfolk, California, in December 1977. He had been discussing reincarnation with the barmaid of a club in town.

The woman had first told him she had been a canary in her previous life. The next time she returned to earth, she told

Redland, she would be a buffalo.

'I admit that I laughed in her face,' the witness said. 'Greatly to my surprise she then shouted, "You may laugh, but I will prove it." At this she reached under the bar, took out a gun, and shot herself dead.'

*   *   *

A Canadian cabaret entertainer called 'Le Grand Melvin', who dressed as a vampire and performed an act with boa constrictors, missed a trick during his act at La Tuque in Quebec, on 22 August 1978.

One of the 7ft 6in long snakes wrapped itself around the entertainer's neck, and when the club manager saw him turning blue in the face called the police.

'I had to cut off the snake's head,' the manager said later. 'It wasn't a pleasant

thing to do. Unfortunately, "Le Grand Melvin" was already dead.'

*　—　*　　　*

An Australian snooker fan who desperately wanted to have a shot named after him spent years trying to come up with a new variation. In January 1979, Robert Fairtree of Melbourne finally cracked the problem.

He announced the 'Fairtree' which was made by a man suspended over the table with his legs fastened to the ceiling and helium balloons attached to his wrists. Sadly, when Robert gave a demonstration he crashed on to the table and died.

*　　　*　　　*

As a dutiful Chief Justice of New Guinea, Sir William Brown was not averse to visiting the scene of a rather unusual traffic accident which had occurred in Papua in April 1979. He was accompanied by members of the jury and also the accused motorist, Mr Morrie Modela.

While the group stood discussing the events, however, they were suddenly startled by the appearance of a number of local tribesmen who emerged from the trees. They were even more surprised when they attacked Mr Modela and hacked him to death.

*　　*　　*

A Sri Lankan woman's attraction for a snake proved fatal in Trincomalee in 1980. She had raised a cobra in the belief that it was her dead son reincarnated.

On 1 July the snake bit her and she died.

58

Two out-of-work Italians were both desperate to land the job as a waiter which had just come vacant in a Naples restaurant in August 1981. As both Fathir Ziouni, 23, and Lofi Aunadni, 22, were scared the other would land the position, they agreed to fight a knife duel on the lonely beach at Latina, south of Naples—winner to take all.

But neither claimed the vacancy. Fathir died, stabbed through the heart, and Lofi was imprisoned for murder.

*   *   *

Attempts to find the oldest man in Asia in 1982 finally brought to light a 118-year-old Malaysian with the extraordinary name Lebai Omar Bin Datuk Panglima Garang. Nor was that all that was extraordinary about him: he was also living in sin with a teenage girl.

To celebrate his record, the old man

agreed to marry the girl. However, on his return from the wedding ceremony riding a tandem which some well-wishers had given him, with his wife on the front, Lebai Omar fell off and died.

*   *   *

There was an unexpected finale to the screening of some pornographic films in Manila in February 1983, which were being shown to raise money to finance an international film festival in the Philippines.

One man died of a stroke – and another was shot dead by his wife, jealous at the sex scenes he had watched.

*   *   *

A fetish for washing women's hair was the undoing of a 29-year-old Italian, Luigi Longhi, when he was brought before a court in Soenderborg, Denmark, in March 1983.

Luigi was said to have had a life-long craving for female tresses, and was confined indefinitely for strangling Heike Freiheit, a 21-year-old West German hitch-hiker, whom he had tied up and then washed her hair four times before killing her.

*   *   *

Sixteen-stone assistant manager James Ferrozzo was enjoying an off-duty hour with one of his dancers, Teresa Hill, in the topless Condor Club, San Francisco, on the night of 22 November 1983. All the customers had left after a hectic evening, and Ferrozzo lay down on the top of a trick baby grand piano beside the girl.

Inadvertently, a switch was triggered

which caused the piano – normally used
in an erotic cabaret – to be raised up and
down to the ceiling. Unaware of what
was happening until it was too late,
Ferrozzo was squashed to death – only
his bulk saving the young dancer beside
him.

'She was so intoxicated she doesn't
even remember getting on the piano,' a
police officer said afterwards.

*   *   *

During a football final between two
Calcutta teams held in November 1983,
over 30,000 spectators went on the
rampage. Police were called in to stem
the pitch invasion and stop the bloody
fights which broke out all over the
ground. In the riot, one man was shot
dead.

The cause of all the trouble had been
an offside decision given by one of the
linesman.

The most unlikely murder weapon was exhibited in a trial held in Wellington, New Zealand, in April 1984.

Before the court was 53-year-old Malcolm Francis, charged with beating his wife to death with – a frozen sausage. He denied the murder.

*　　*　　*

Olympic marathon hopeful, Richard Mbelwa, 22, of Dar es Salaam in Tanzania, had put in many hours of arduous training. As he was running through a golf course on the morning of 10 May 1984, a policeman suddenly ran into sight and shot him dead.

The officer said later he thought Mbelwa was a fleeing thief.

*　　*　　*

Turkish authorities decided to ban the screening of video tapes in buses after a tragedy in Ankara, in June 1984.

An offended bus driver had tried to turn off a love scene on a video while he was driving along. In the ensuing accident seventeen people were killed.

* * *

Two Chicago lawyers arguing the respective merits of certain athletes in forthcoming Olympic Games in July 1984 decided to settle their dispute by racing each other down a hallway in their law firm.

One of the men, who had poor eyesight, crashed through a 39th-floor window and fell to his death.

* * *

An Italian with an eye for beautiful girls could not resist the temptation offered by a private nudist beach near his home in Naples. One day in July 1984, 48-year-old Salvatore Ancoretti climbed up to a rock high above the beach and with his binoculars oggled the nude sunbathers below.

In his excitement, though, he forgot to check the rock for safety – and when it gave way he plunged 100 feet to the beach. He died on impact – still clutching his binoculars.

*　　　*　　　*

A 34-year-old Yugoslav, Vebi Limani, died near his home on Sara Mountain in August 1984 when he was struck by lightning.

Reporting his death, the local newspaper *Politika* said he was the fourth member of his family to die in the

past six years. His father, brother and uncle had all passed on – similarly struck dead by lightning.

*   *   *

Three parachutists attempted a spectacular trick jump before thousands of spectators in Denver, Colorado, in August 1984. They were planning to float to the ground one above the other.

Instead, the top man dropped on the parachute of the man below and both fell on the third jumper. All three were killed.

*   *   *

Barbecuing was one of the passions shared by Diane Fellman and her

husband, Jim, at their palatial American home in San Jose.

But when they fell out of love in August 1984, Diane shot poor Jim. Afterward she cooked his body on the barbecue and ate part of his arm.

*   *   *

There was a curious sequel to a murder case in Los Angeles in September 1984. A mother of 61 who had buried her murdered son the previous year instituted proceedings against the police claiming damages of $500,000.

She claimed that the law still had her boy's skull.

*   *   *

Torrential rain had left hundreds of Indians homeless in the Assam area, and they waited with increasing anxiety for relief supplies in September 1984.

When a helicopter finally reached the flood victims to make a drop, two people were killed and three others injured when they were hit by the falling food packets.

*　　　*　　　*

Fifty-seven-year-old Edward Hill was feeling pretty chipper as he left a Houston hospital in November 1984. He had just spent three weeks being treated for a minor heart complaint and was now declared fit.

As he crossed the foyer he was handed his bill for the treatment. He took one look — and dropped dead. The bill was for $38,000!

3

IN MEMORIAM

Over the years there have been some very apt and often humorous comments passed 'In Memoriam'. Here are some of the best of them.

The most bizarre final comment was surely that of a convicted English murderer, Edgar Edwards, as he was led to the scaffold in December 1902, condemned to death for killing John and Beatrice Darby.

As he mounted the steps, he said brightly to the hangman, 'I've been looking forward to this!'

* * *

Two American Army buddies were chopping wood together on fatigue duty at Fort Smith, Arkansas, in June 1922. Suddenly, Private Daniel McGranie remembered that his friend, Private Benjamin Clark, owed him ten dollars. He demanded the money back there and then.

Both men stopped chopping and an argument ensued. Clark denied ever having borrowed the money and refused McGranie's insistent demands.

All at once McGranie lifted his axe and with one blow severed his friend's head from his body.

'I just lost my head,' was all he could mutter as he was taken in charge.

*　　　*　　　*

A deranged New Yorker, Ernest Walker, not only committed a totally motiveless crime in 1949, but also left an equally

bizarre confession at the scene of the crime.

Walker lured a young messenger boy to his Manhattan apartment and clubbed him to death with an iron poker. He then left the body for the police to find with a note scrawled upon it:

'I expect you will be surprised to see what I have done.'

*   *   *

Police were somewhat baffled when they were called to the Ministry of Tourism Offices in Nairobi, Kenya, in June 1959, by a distraught clerk who said that a man was savagely attacking a *stuffed* lion.

The officers arrived to find the man pummelling the lion and shrieking abuse. He had apparently smashed the glass cage in which it was on display and then tried to strangle it.

Said one of the policemen later,

'When the man calmed down he told us his brother had been killed by a lion and he wanted revenge!'

*   *   *

Mischievous little 3-year-old George Semple was being taken for a walk along the cliffs at Brighton, in Sussex, by a family friend in 1960, when he tumbled over and was killed on the rocks below.

Later, the friend confessed to the police that she was responsible, having pushed George over. 'He just would not behave,' she said.

*   *   *

Few learner drivers showed more determination than Mr David George of

Shanklin, in the Isle of Wight. Then immediately upon being told he had passed his test in July 1976, he collapsed over the wheel of his car and died.

'It was his eighth attempt,' a sad instructor said later.

*   *   *

Another man who had success snatched from his grasp at the moment of triumph was an American, Johann Crispet of Washington, who died in August 1976 on the day before he was due to be awarded a licence to practise law. What was also remarkable about Mr Crispet was that he was 102 years old.

'He always wanted to practise at the bar,' said his son later. 'Before he died he had taken the requisite examinations twenty-six times!'

*   *   *

In order to emphasise the terrible nature
of hanging, D.H. Beenan, a leading
opponent of capital punishment, was
demonstrating just what happened
when it took place to an audience in New
Zealand, in 1976.

Slipping a noose which he had
hanging from a rafter around his neck,
Mr Beenan exclaimed, 'How horrible the
whole thing is!' – stepped from the chair
he was standing upon and accidentally
hanged himself.

* * *

As he was taking photographs of the city
dump of Takapuna, also in New Zealand,
for a new brochure in July 1976,
photographer Peter Hammond became
conscious of a bulldozer coming in his
direction. Anxious not to interrupt the
driver's work, Mr Hammond stepped
behind a pile of rubbish.

At this – said a policeman later giving evidence into Mr Hammond's death – the bulldozer driver brought his vehicle closer and with incredible delicacy squashed the photographer into the ground.

The driver later told the law, 'I hate snoopers.'

*　　*　　*

In February 1977, a West German housewife, Hilda Brunner of Frankfurt, was charged with murdering her husband by putting rat poison in his daily glass of beer for a period of four years.

She confessed to the police, 'I only did it to cure him of drinking.'

*　　*　　*

75

It was an open and shut case when Michael Koukourakis appeared before a court in Piraeus, Greece, in September 1977, charged with murdering his wife's lover.

Michael was very ready to admit he shot the man to death, but pleaded, 'I acted in an instant of momentary sanity.'

The jury agreed and acquitted him.

*　　*　　*

When a group of Brazilian policemen raided a party in Santiago after complaints that it had been going on noisily for three days in May 1978, they found rather more than they expected. For sitting upright in one corner was a dead man.

Asked to explain, the host of the party said, 'He was a gate-crasher called Jose. We discovered that he was dead on Saturday evening. But not wanting to spoil the party we decided to leave him there until Monday morning.'

French farmer Pierre Trichard of Mexmieux was happily watching a game of World Cup football on television in June 1978 when his wife, Claudi, asked him to shell some peas for their supper.

Pierre refused, and despite several further entreaties, continued to stare resolutely at the TV set. At this, Claudi snatched her husband's shotgun from the wall, took aim, and blew his head off.

'I couldn't understand it,' Mme Trichard said later, 'France were already out of the competition.'

* * *

Football also shattered the happy home life of a Yugoslavian couple in August 1982. While Marinko Janevski, a retired policeman, was watching a match on TV at his home in Belgrade, his wife came into the room and tried to stop him.

'I strangled her,' Marinko later

admitted while standing trial for murder. 'I always get excited when watching football.'

* * *

While Mrs Barbara Eastman was selling flowers in Naysmith Square, Toronto, in September 1978, she was suddenly approached by a man who announced: 'I am God – could you direct me to the nearest church, please?'

Although somewhat taken aback, Mrs Eastman gave the necessary instructions and then watched in amazement at what happened next – for as she later explained in court:

'When I had given him the directions he took off his hat, said "Thank you", stepped out into the road, and was instantly killed by a tractor.'

* * *

All his life, keen angler Jerry Head of Melbourne, Australia, had dreamed of catching a giant-size fish. When he did, it literally killed him – as his wife Rhoda told newpapermen in November 1978, after the family had marked his passing in a rather unusual way.

'He was out fishing with my son Doug when he landed a 58-pound cod.' said Mrs Head. 'The shock killed him. But after the funeral we had a fish supper – cod-fritters on a bed of clams with his name written in instant potato over the lot.'

*   *   *

After the unfortunate death of her father, Mrs Joan Spence gave evidence at a London inquest in March 1980.

'My father died after slipping on a bacon sandwich,' she told the court. 'As he was a life-long vegetarian I consider this to be a manifestation of divine injustice.'

The familiar situation of a husband falling out with his mother-in-law took on a new dimension in India, in April 1980.

For when Vekay Velayudhan appeared in a court in Poona charged with beheading his mother-in-law, he said simply in his defence: 'We had not been getting along for some time.'

*   *   *

Problems can also arise between parents and children – but hardly as bizarre as that which occurred in America, in October 1980. Before a New York juvenile court appeared 14-year-old Christine Martin who said that because her parents had complained when her pet rabbit left droppings on their living-room carpet, she picked up her father's gun and shot them both to death.

'I have been having problems with them for some time,' she calmly added.

Mr Harry Olsen was understandably upset at the death of his wife, the former Miss Stella Walsh, an Olympic Gold and Bronze Medallist, who passed away at their home in southern California in December 1980.

But he was stunned by the revelation of the post-mortem that his 'wife' was, in fact, a man!

'We had been married for almost thirty years,' he said afterwards. 'I am 92, but I must have been a lot more innocent then than now.'

*   *   *

The 'shooting' of arch-villain J.R. Ewing in the television soap opera 'Dallas' provoked as many heated arguments as to who was responsible both on-screen as well as off. In Dallas itself, in March 1981, a couple named Silverstone took their argument to the limit in a grim

reprise of the show itself.

So angry did the wife become at her husband's refusal to agree with her verdict on who was JR's killer, that she walked out of the living room, fetched a shotgun, and slayed her husband.

'She was under some strain,' a relative told police later.

*   *   *

A South African judge with the singularly appropriate name of Justice W.J. Human was addressing a man who had been found guilty of rape, in August 1983.

Sentencing the prisoner, Rodney Axe, to death, he added, 'I have treated you as leniently as possible.'

*   *   *

82

At an inquest in Sheffield, Yorkshire, in October 1983, into the death of a Mr Harry Tanner, evidence was given by his brother who had watched the whole incident.

John Tanner said that his brother had climbed to the top of a 200-foot high bridge and then with a wave of his hand and a shout of 'Geronimo!' had plunged to his death in the river Tees.

'He was a happy-go-lucky chap,' added Mr Tanner.

*　　*　　*

A quickstep became a 'danse macabre' in a fashionable Dallas nightspot called Ianni's Club, in May 1984, when a man became enraged. For no apparent reason, the dancer shot his partner and then went on a spree killing five more people.

A police spokesman said later, 'He

pulled a pistol and shot several people.
He left, went to his car, reloaded, came
back and shot some more!'

*   *   *

Faces were red in Fort Lauderdale,
Florida, when a letter was sent out by the
local social security office in June 1984
to a woman of 61 who had died the
previous December.

The letter, to a Mrs Pat Shamres, six
months after her death, contained a
handwritten addition which said, 'We
have received a report that you may be
deceased. Please come in with proof of
identity.'

*   *   *

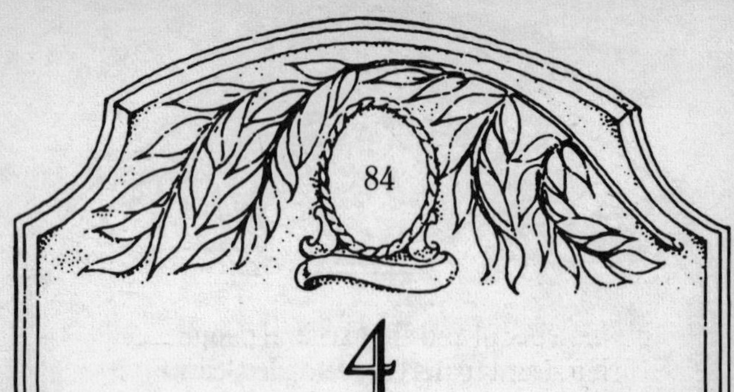

4

EXIT LINES

And now a few last words from the famous, beginning perhaps inevitably with Oscar Wilde (1854–1900) who, true to his reputation, is credited with not one but two exit lines on his death-bed. So you may take your choice from either.

'This wallpaper is killing me. One of us must go.'

Or else:

'Alas, I am dying beyond my means.'

* * *

The great South African statesman, Cecil Rhodes (1853–1902), took his final confinement with ill-concealed annoyance and his final words were to one of his secretaries:

'Turn me over, Jack.'

*   *   *

The enormously influential Russian playwright, Anton Chekhov (1860–1904), who died at the height of his powers had a suitably dry comment to make:

'It's a long time since I drank champagne.'
(Appropriately, the great man's coffin then rode to burial in a freight car marked FRESH OYSTERS!)

*   *   *

The brilliant American short story writer, O. Henry (real name William Sydney Porter, 1862–1910), went out of this vale of tears quoting from a popular song:

'Turn up the lights. I don't want to go home in the dark.'

*   *   *

Efforts to make the great Russian writer and mystic, Leo Tolstoy (1828–1910), seek comfort from the Russian Orthodox Church as he lay on his death-bed were met with this sharp rejoinder – which was also his last:

'Even in the valley of the shadow of death, two and two do not make six.'

*   *   *

The energetic 26th President of the
United States Theodore Roosevelt
(1858–1919), slipped gracefully away
with these words to those grouped
around his bed:
  'Put out the light.'

    *   *   *

Robert Erskine Childers (1870–1922),
author of the classic spy thriller, *Riddle
of the Sands* (1903) and a member of
Sinn Fein, said, as he was about to be
executed, with other patriots, by an Irish
Free State firing squad:
  'Take a step or two forwards, lads – it
will be easier that way.'

    *   *   *

The famous English novelist, Arnold Bennett (1867–1931), died in Paris of typhoid after drinking a glass of water. His last words were:

'The water is perfectly safe.'

* * *

Thomas Edison (1847–1931), the American inventor and man of vision, chose to look forward rather than back in his last words, informing those around his death-bed with tantalising emphasis:

'It's very beautiful over there.'

* * *

Oliver Wendell Holmes (1841–1935), the great American judge, delighted in telling the story of the last moments of one of his uncles, John Holmes, who died in Boston. As the man lay on his death-bed, a nurse who was busy keeping his feet warm was heard to remark, 'If his feet are warm, he is alive — nobody ever died with his feet warm.'

At this, John Holmes suddenly sat up in bed and said, 'John Rogers did!' Then he died.

(John Rogers was an English Protestant burned at the stake for heresy in 1555.)

*   *   *

One of the finest British men of the law of this century, Lord Chief Justice Gordon Hewart (1870–1944), passed away on a fine spring morning with these words ringing around his room:

'Damn it! There's that cuckoo again!'

The irrascible film comedian and life-long agnostic W.C. Fields (1880–1946) was found reading the Bible on his death-bed. Asked the reason for this astonishing about-face, Fields grumbled:

'I'm looking for a loop-hole!'

*   *   *

One of the funniest men of the twentieth century, humorist James Thurber (1894–1961), who shrugged off the blindness that inflicted his last years with comments like, 'I don't get distracted by the sight of a pretty girl – but of course I can still *hear* a pretty girl go by,' did not disappoint his admirers with his last words:

'God bless . . . God damn!'

*   *   *

The rumbustious Irish writer and notorious drinker, Brendan Behan (1923–64), passed his last remark to a nun comforting him on his death-bed:

   'Ah, bless you Sister, may all your sons be Bishops.'

*   *   *

When the pioneer woman Member of Parliament and socialite, Nancy Astor (1879–1964), found herself surrounded by her children as she lay dying in her bed she demanded of them:

   'Am I dying or is this my birthday?'

*   *   *

Tallulah Bankhead (1903–68), the American actress and a celebrated wit, was economic in her use of words and amusing in her demand when she died in New York City's St Luke's Hospital.

'Bourbon,' she said.

*　　*　　*

That master of wit and humour, Sir Noel Coward (1899–1976), did not disappoint his friends and admirers when it came to making his final *bon mot:*

'Goodnight, my darlings, I'll see you tomorrow,' he said.

*　　*　　*

'The King of Rock 'n' Roll', Elvis Presley
(1935–77), despite the torment of his
closing years remained a devout
Christian to the end, and his last remark
was singularly appropriate:
'We'll make this tour the best ever.'

*   *   *

American Pulitzer prize-winning author
William Saroyan (1908–81) actually
went to the trouble of telephoning the
Associated Press with what were to be his
last words:
'Everybody has got to die, but I have
always believed an exception would be
made in my case. Now what?'

*   *   *

The distinguished British comic actor, John Le Mesurier (1912–83), employed his gentle, irreverent sense of humour when he left instructions for the following announcement of his death to be published in the Personal Column of *The Times* newspaper:

'JOHN LE MESURIER wishes it to be known that he conked out on November 15th. He sadly misses family and friends.'

*   *   *

The famous English comedian and magician, Tommy Cooper (1922–84), who collapsed and died while appearing on stage during a live television show, passed on joking just as he had done in life.

At the end of his act he held up a black square of rubber and said, 'This is an Irishman's bowling ball.'

And as the audience chuckled, he ad-libbed, 'I thought it would get a bigger laugh than that.' It was the last joke he ever made.

As Oscar Wilde opened this section with two exit lines, it is perhaps only appropriate to close in the same manner – though it is equally open to debate whether the humorist in question used either remark attributed to him.

Much-loved comedian Eric Morecambe (1926–84) said in February 1981 that he would like to be remembered as a skilful fisherman and hoped his last words would reflect this.

'I don't talk much about it now,' he said, 'because I blush easily. But I hope people in the future will appreciate my genius – particularly with pilchards – and how I beat the handicap of having an apprentice with short and hairy gumboots.'

In November 1983, after he had twice overcome heart attacks he was again asked how he would like his obituary to read. Eric replied with characteristic speed:

"See, I told you!"

*   *   *

5

GHASTLY SPIRITS

The goings-on of those who have passed over can also have their funny side as the spirited stories in this section will show.

Take, for example, the amorous ghost who began paying his attentions to a pretty, 18-year-old Manchester girl, Sarah James, in March 1965. According to Sarah, her invisible lover would announce himself to her as she lay in bed with a gentle kiss on the shoulder. Then she would feel the touch of his hands on her body under the bedclothes, and finally the sensation of someone getting into bed.

'I just let him do what he wants,' Sarah declared. 'And he does it beautifully . . . he can certainly love!'

But when Sarah's mother, Jane, grew alarmed at these stories and decided to

change places with her daughter and sleep in her bed . . . nothing happened.

The randy wraith preferred blondes, it was decided.

*   *   *

The doctors at a New York hospital were amazed when a 41-year-old patient, Donald Cohen, suddenly leapt out of his bed in March 1968. Their amazement was understandable: Donald had had two heart attacks and the specialists had given him up for dead.

But that wasn't the only amazing thing about his recovery. He had a bizarre story to recount of his experiences 'on the other side'.

'I dreamt I was on a merry-go-round,' he said, 'and the angel of death was beckoning me. The carousel picked up speed, but I managed to resist the mysterious force that pulled me towards him.

'I jumped off – and found myself on the floor of the hospital ward!'

A Swedish doctor has devised the strangest set of scales imaginable, according to a report published in 1969. Dr Nils Olof Jacobson believed it was possible to weigh the human soul and set about proving his theory by placing the hospital beds of dying patients on extremely sensitive scales.

From his research, said Dr Jacobson, he had established that at the precise moment of death the scales registered a decrease of just eight-tenths of an ounce!

* * *

Ugandan witch doctor, Dada M'Shuma, became famous throughout his country in the 1970s as 'The Man Who Can See The Future'. The old man was said to be able to make contact with the dead and also predict events that were to come.

Millions were said to believe implicity

in Dada, according to a report – but
sceptics claimed he got his knowledge of
world affairs from a transistor radio
hidden in his hut . . .

*   *   *

Anton Kjowski, a Polish immigrant who
lived in Manchester, was obsessed with
an ancient superstition that he had
brought with him from the 'old country'
he left over a quarter of a century earlier.
He believed in vampires.

And because the traditional method of
guarding against attack from vampires
was to keep plenty of garlic about the
house, Anton doubled his defences by
sleeping with a clove of garlic in his
mouth. Tragically, he was wracked by
coughing one night in April 1973,
dislodged the piece of garlic, and was
choked to death by the clove.

According to a 'Vampire Census' carried out by the Vampire Research Centre in New York in April 1983, there are thirty-five people in the United States who consider themselves to belong to the ranks of the Living Undead.

Of these people, a third lived in the state of California and one is an alien vampire – having emigrated from Spain.

*　　*　　*

A ghost with a fascination for sexy movies made his presence felt in a cinema in Bury, Lancashire, in 1976. Nicknamed, 'Old Sid', the spectre had a habit of appearing whenever X-rated films were shown.

'Old Sid' had been seen around the cinema for many years – but less in recent times until the advent of more explicit movies. Several times he was spotted dressed in medieval clothes and a three-cornered hat, hovering about six feet over the stalls.

Apparently what 'Old Sid' *didn't* like were horror movies . . .

* * *

Halfway through a séance on the top floor of the Spiritualists' Association headquarters in London, in March 1978, an insistent tapping was heard from outside a blacked-out window. Then a voice asked, 'Can I come in?'

The medium holding the séance promptly asked the spirit's name and a voice replied, 'Ken.'

For a moment there was a puzzled silence among those taking part in the séance, and then the voice spoke again: 'I've been repairing the roof and somebody's locked the window on me. Let me in!'

At this everyone present collapsed into laughter, said secretary Tom Johanson later, and the 'ghost' was promptly let in from 'the other side'.

*　　　*　　　*

'Fred', the ghost who was reported to be haunting the Sapsford family of Larkfield, Kent, in August 1978, was a rather unusual kind of spirit — a high

spirit, in fact. For according to the four people he suffered from B.O.

For fourteen years, the Sapsfords had been aware of 'Fred' who usually made his presence felt by the unmistakable odour of sweaty feet. At other times he left behind the scent of sizzling bacon, burnt toast and roast coffee.

Said Mrs Joan Sapsford, 'We don't want him exorcised – just sanitised.'

*   *   *

The Ghost family come in for a fair amount of joking. In fact there are several people with the name of Ghost, and one, Mrs Violet Ghost of London said in 1979:

'We get a lot of phone calls from people taking the mickey. They ask if we could pop round and haunt a house for them. Some even ask if we really *are* spooks. Even my doctor used to sing "Holy, Holy, Holy" when he saw me coming!'

One relative changed his name by deed poll to get away from all these jokes, added Mrs Ghost. 'He was a solicitor and had to put up with a lot of laughter in court!'

But she still thinks it's a splendid name. 'When I'm introduced to people they always remember me. They never forget having spoken to a Ghost!'

* * *

A ghost found his way into a court in Albany, New York, in September 1979 — if only in spirit.

A couple, who were being sued for reneging on an agreement to purchase an old house built in 1857, claimed they changed their minds after discovering the place was haunted.

In the interim, however, new purchasers had been found: although they had so far seen nothing, it was reported. But they *were* anxious for an encounter, as the man explained.

'We hope its the kind of ghost that moves furniture around for we could sure use the help!'

*   *   *

Another ghost made its presence felt in a court in Palm Beach, Florida, a few months later in January 1980.

Things began to go bump in the night after a 56-year-old millionaire shot himself in Jim and Corinne Succhi's villa, the court was told. Explained Jim, 'The doors opened and shut, water taps started to gush, electric lights flashed on and off, and at midnight we were roused by terrifying screams.

He and his wife were suing the millionaire's heirs for $100,000, claiming they suffered fear and sleepless nights in the haunted home.

Defending the case for the heirs, attorney James Waters said, 'I've heard of paying guests, but not paying ghosts. Even if it's true that my dead client haunts the house, he has every right to spook where he pleases.'

And the judge agreed.

A Californian mystic, Sande Marsolan, founded a Ghost Adoption Society, in Feburary 1980, offering clients the chance to become friends with famous spirits from the past such as Shakespeare and (can you believe it?) Attila the Hun!

According to Ms Marsolan, she has had the gift to communicate with ghosts since she was five, but it takes her three hours of intense concentration to reach specific spirits. Among the eighty-five spirits she had called up was a beautiful female ghost from the Renaissance era who shared the prison cell of a man in San Quentin – that is until she began playing tricks on the guards!

For her $150 fee she also made contact with the ghost of the Marquis de Sade who was wanted to 'liven things up' in a Los Angeles hair saloon.

Unfortunately, Ms Marsolan had to be hastily summoned back to get rid of the randy Marquis when he apparently began a persistent bout of pinching the bottoms of the young girl assistants!

This same year also saw another 'spirited' offer made to American believers in the supernatural.

The May 1980 issue of a spiritualist magazine said that astral love-making was now available. For $1,000, a group of mediums offered clients a chance to once again make love to partners who had passed on!

*   *   *

When the President of Italy's Magicians' Association, Antonio Battista, lost £1,000 in cash, a camera and over 200 letters from clients, from his car in January 1982 he took immediate action against the thieves.

Antonio had large warnings posted up on hoardings all over the town of Avellino in southern Italy where the robbery had ocurred. These told the

culprits that unless the stolen items were returned within three days, then he would work his magic and put the 'Evil Eye' on them.

Twenty-four hours later, Battista's magic *had* worked – but not completely. The letters were returned safely wrapped up in a plastic bag. But the thieves kept the camera and the cash!

* * *

In June 1982, two American psychics claimed that it was the spirit of Adolf Hitler that had masterminded the Argentine invasion of the Falkland Islands.

The men claimed that the one-time Fuehrer of the Third Reich had not lost his 'insane drive for world domination' and was doing his best to influence conflicts where ever he could find them.

The psychics said they had learned all
this from seeing visions of Hitler who
was being kept active in his after-life by
hormones!

*   *   *

A wave of fear spread over the Inkomazi
district of the Transvaal in the autumn of
1982 when the emaciated figure of
Lamkhtswa Mhlongo was suddenly seen
about the area after an absence of
seventeen years. It was generally
believed that Mhlongo had been eaten by
a crocodile so that this must surely be
his ghost!

At last, one brave man approached the
'spirit'.

'Oh, no, I'm not a ghost,' the other
grinned. 'I've been in Swaziland – I ran
away to become a witch doctor!'

*   *   *

For almost a year it wasn't the thought of the treatment that they might get in a West German dentist's surgery that terrified his patients — but the possibility of being haunted by a ghost named 'Chopper'.

According to reports, 'Chopper' — who was never actually seen — would shout insults in a staccato voice at patients sitting in the surgery at Neutraubling in Bavaria. These remarks would issue from power points, light fittings or even pieces of surgical equipment. Sometimes the words the spirit used were highly suggestive in tone.

But the loquacious phantom turned out to be an elaborate hoax. And in December 1983, 62-year-old dentist Dr Kurt Bachseitz was fined DM 12,400 in a local court for staging the trick. His 17-year-old assistant, Claudia Judenmann, had been the 'voice' of 'Chopper'.

*   *   *

Just to close on a cheerful note – there's love and sex after death according to an American ghost hunter named Stanley Wojcik of New Jersey. He revealed in 1984 that ghosts engage in love-making just like ordinary mortals, and also go to the cinema, like to ride in cars and aeroplanes, and even enjoy parties!

'Spirits are just like human beings,' he said his research had shown. 'They are the astral counterparts of their former mortal selves. Sex after death is not biological. Spirits *do* make love, but it's an all-cellular love – a blending of their energies!'

THE END

(Or is it?)